This book belongs to:

_____

_____

To the Su Songs, Zhang Hengs, and Cai Luns of the 21st century.
- P.A.

To newlyweds, such as my niece Jessica and cousin-in-law Tina: bon voyage!
- O.C.

To Juan Agustin and Mateo.
- J.C.

Immedium, Inc.
P.O. Box 31846
San Francisco, CA 94131
www.immedium.com

www.liberumdonum.com

First hardcover edition published 2018.

Edited by Don Menn
  Book design by Joy Liu-Trujillo

Printed in Malaysia
  10 9 8 7 6 5 4 3 2 1

Library of Congress Cataloging-in-Publication Data

Names: Amara, Phil, author. | Chin, Oliver Clyde, 1969- author. | Calle, Juan, 1977- illustrator.

Title: The discovery of fireworks and gunpowder / by Phil Amara & Oliver Chin; illustrated by Juan Calle.

Description: First hardcover edition. | San Francisco : Immedium, Inc., 2018. | Series: The Asian hall of fame |
  Summary: "Dao, a red panda, guides Ethan and Emma, two school children, back into time to discover how
  gunpowder was created in China and how fireworks became popular worldwide"-- Provided by publisher.

Identifiers: LCCN 2018014290 (print) | LCCN 2018021001 (ebook) | ISBN 9781597021449 (ebook) | ISBN 9781597021425 (hardcover)

Subjects: | CYAC: Time travel--Fiction. | Gunpowder--Fiction. | Fireworks--Fiction. | Red panda--Fiction. | Pandas--Fiction.
  | China--History--Song dynasty, 960-1279--Fiction.

Classification: LCC PZ7.A49153 (ebook) | LCC PZ7.A49153 Din 2018 (print) | DDC [E]--dc23

LC record available at https://lccn.loc.gov/2018014290

ISBN: 978-1-59702-142-5

The Discovery of
# FIREWORKS & GUNPOWDER

## The Asian Hall of Fame

烟花和火药的发现

immedium

Immedium, Inc.
San Francisco, CA

by Phil Amara & Oliver Chin

Illustrated by Juan Calle

On the weekend, Ethan and Emma were exploring downtown. Pop! "What's that noise?" asked Ethan.

POP

POP
POP

Pop! Pop!
"It's coming from over there,"
said Emma.

They hurried up the street
and through the gate.

The pair poked through a crowd. A shopkeeper lit a string of small red tubes. Pop! Pop! Pop! Suddenly dozens of flashes, puffs of smoke, and a shower of paper sprinkled the sidewalk.

POP
POP
POP

"Firecrackers!" shouted Ethan.

"How do fireworks work?"
wondered Emma.

POP

ASIA

"I'm glad you asked!" said a
cute red panda who appeared before them.
"I'm Dao You, your guide to amazing things from Asia."

The kids were thunderstruck!

"Fireworks came from gunpowder. Their story sparkles with surprises... and danger," hinted Dao. "Gunpowder, paper, printing, and the compass are called China's Four Great Inventions."

"Cool, tell me more!" said Ethan.

Emma asked, "Can you show us where this powder came from?"

POP

"Buckle your seatbelts," answered Dao.
Their furry friend hit a small gong with a mallet.
Gooone! They vanished in the blink of an eye.

The three time travelers landed on a stone bridge. "Chang-an was one of China's Seven Ancient Capitals," said Dao. "In the year 1 CE the Han Dynasty thought wood, fire, earth, metal, and water were the key parts of nature."

"Alchemists were like scientists. They investigated how the five elements interacted," Dao continued. "But as Taoists, they wanted to transform these substances and find a golden elixir — a potion for eternal life."

Linna noted, "Legends said throwing bamboo into a fire scared away mountain beasts."

"Man-made thunder and lightning!" said Ethan.

"Pursuing a magic pill, alchemists discovered how to make bigger bangs!" added Dao.

"What does a fire need?" asked Dao.

Emma answered, "Fuel, heat, and oxygen."

Dao said, "Yes! The Chinese learned that three materials could fan fire's flames."

a yellow mineral that burned and smelled of rotten eggs

HEAT

CHARCOAL

SULFUR

burned wood

OXYGEN

SALTPETER

FUEL

a white crust from decaying organisms or dung

Zip! The trio zoomed to 1044. Alchemists ground, mixed, and heated these items together. They found the recipe: 2 parts sulfur, 3 parts charcoal, and 15 parts saltpeter. The Chinese word for gunpowder is "fire medicine."

火药

POOF

The first fireworks were bamboo tubes
filled with black powder.
The Chinese word for firecracker
means "exploding bamboo."

But chemistry explains the
chain reaction happening inside.

爆竹

The sulfur burns first at a low temperature.
Next the fire is fueled by charcoal.
Then the saltpeter releases oxygen
to boost the fire.

Heated gas rapidly expands with destructive force.
This truly was the power of the heavens!

Emma thought, "Since black powder blew things up, people could use it to mine and build roads."

Ethan guessed, "But also to fight?"

BOOM!!!

"Fighting isn't the path to immortality," sighed Dao. "Follow me and be careful." Zap!

"This is 1132 in Kaifeng, another one of China's old capitals," announced Dao. "Here the Song Dynasty experimented. They put black powder on birds, oxen, carts, and arrows and launched them toward their foes."

There were four ways to channel gunpowder on the battlefield.
1) Spray the fire out.
The Song attached bamboo packed with powder
onto spears to make fire lances.

Ethan cried,
"The first flamethrower!"

2) Seal it in a container with a fuse.
The harder the shell, the more damaging the explosion.

Bamboo was replaced by paper, leather, and then metal.

This was the bomb.

Zap! "Now we're in 1232," Dao whispered.
"The Jin Dynasty defended Kaifeng against Genghis Khan's invading Mongols."

The Jin named one of
their fearsome devices the
"heaven-shaking-thunder bomb."

Since the dawn of time, people could only throw objects.
Now they could use another source of energy.

3) Exploding gas could propel bombs far distances.

This was the rocket or missile.

4) Lastly one could ignite the powder in a tube,
and the explosion would shoot an object.

This was the gun.

Cannons changed how wars were fought
on land and soon at sea.

The secret of gunpowder traveled to Europe. In 1267 English friar Roger Bacon recorded the formula in a book to the Pope. In 1295 traveler Marco Polo returned home to Venice, Italy and wrote about his experiences in China.

The cannon was followed by the pistol and rifle. Discoveries of "smokeless" gunpowder propelled mightier weapons on earth, through water, and in the air.

"However, let's see how fireworks developed," suggested Dao.

"Off the battlefield, fireworks were used in other rituals," stated Dao.

"They scare away bad spirits and insects," proposed Ethan.

"That's good at birthdays, weddings, funerals, and holidays," said Emma.

Emma observed, "Along with gunpowder, fireworks spread around the world."

"Everyone likes to party!" said Ethan.

"But setting them off is dangerous, so watch out!" warned Dao.

"Fireworks may entertain a crowd, but safety should always come first,"
Dao cautioned. "In England during the Middle Ages, fire masters had assistants
called 'green men' who wore leaves to shield them from the sparks."

"How did fireworks get their colors?" wondered Emma.

Dao answered, "In 1777 when Americans first celebrated their July 4th Independence Day, the only color was orange!"

"But in the 1830s Italians adjusted their gunpowder recipe to make it burn much hotter," Dao continued.

"They injected their powder with metallic salts, which could now burn in the blast to make different colors."

"How did fireworks get their shapes?" asked Ethan.

"Metallic powder is packed into balls called 'stars' and arranged in the gunpowder in special patterns," Dao replied. "In a mortar, the lift charge ignites to launch the shell up to 300 miles an hour, more than 1,000 feet high."

"A fuse inside the shell burns slowly and triggers a burst charge. The shell explodes!" explained Dao. "Stars fly and flare into colorful flickers of light. Metallic salts also provide the sounds: the screech, whistle, and bang."

Today a pyrotechnician programs a computerized remote control to fire electronically and coordinate with music and laser light shows.

There are many types of aerial shells, such as Round, Palm, Chrysanthemum, and Serpentine.

"Stadiums feature fireworks after a game," noted Ethan.

"Amusement parks send them to say good night!" added Emma.

"That reminds me, it's time for you to go back home,"
yelped Dao. He hit his gong. Gooone!

They instantly returned downtown! "Modern fireworks make designs that the ancient Chinese could only have dreamed of," Dao laughed. "But China remains the largest manufacturer of firecrackers in the world."

Meanwhile the neighborhood buzzed with excitement.
"The festival is getting started," yelled Ethan.

"Dao, can you stay?" asked Emma.

"Sure thing!" replied Dao.
"I'm the biggest fan of
fireworks there is!"

# GLOSSARY

**Alchemy** — early form of chemistry whose goal was to create gold or a magical elixir.

**Aerial Shell** — a type of fireworks shell shot by a mortar; it contains a fuse, lift charge, stars, and a burst charge.

**Bamboo** — green, fast-growing species of grass whose tall woody stems are hollow; favorite food of pandas.

**Burst Charge** — part of an aerial shell that explodes to spread a colored pattern of fireworks.

**Chang-an** — one of the seven capitals of ancient China, now called Xian.

**Charcoal** — lightweight blackened leftovers after organic matter loses water (ex. when wood burns without oxygen).

**Chemistry** — a branch of science that investigates elements and their properties and how they interact.

**Chrysanthemum** — circular shaped flower, cultivated in China since the 15th century BCE.

**Dynasty** — a series of rulers who came from the same family, clan, or ethnic group.

**Elixir** — an alchemist's magical formula to produce gold or provide eternal life.

**Firecracker** — a small paper cylinder that contains explosive material that can be lit by a fuse.

**Fuse** — cord that burns to ignite an explosive.

**Genghis Khan** — (1162-1227) led Mongols to rule the largest land empire in world history.

**Gunpowder** — the first known chemical explosive, composed of charcoal, saltpeter, and sulfur.

**Han Dynasty** — Second imperial rulers of China (206 BCE–220 CE).

**Jin Dynasty** — also known as the Jurchen (1115-1234), second great "barbarian" rulers of northern China.

**Kaifeng** — one of the seven capitals of ancient China, located in the Henan province.

**Lance** — spear used by horse-riding soldiers (cavalry) for combat.

**Lift Charge** — bottom part of an aerial shell that ignites first to propel it high into the sky.

**Marco Polo** — Italian (1254-1324) who traveled to Asia (1271-1295) and met Genghis Khan's grandson Kublai.

**Mongols** — nomadic barbarians from Mongolia led by Genghis Khan. Famed for their archery and horse riding.

**Mortar** — a short cannon that can fire shells at high angles into the air.

**Oxygen** — (element O, atomic number 8) needed by most organisms to live and by fire to burn.

**Pyrotechnician** — a fireworks specialist (or "artist or craftsman of fire").

**Saltpeter** — potassium nitrate, residue from bacteria which decay organic material.

**Star** — a small pack of metallic compounds that produce specific fireworks colors and patterns.

**Song Dynasty** — Chinese rulers (960-1279) whose capital was located at Kaifeng, and who developed gunpowder.

**Sulfur** — a yellow powder (element S, atomic number 16) that smells when burned.

**Taoism** — Chinese philosophy (4th century BCE) that values living in harmony with nature.

Fun Fact: Disney patented a system using compressed air to launch fireworks and reduce air and noise pollution.